TRUTH *OR* BUSTED

WORLD WAR ONE MADE SOLDIERS' ← FEET GO ROTTEN!

The fact or fiction behind BATTLES & WARS

...ay Barnham

WAYLAND

First published in paperback in 2015 by Wayland

Dewey Number: 355'.02-dc23
ISBN: 978 0 7502 9619 9
eBook ISBN: 978 0 7502 8728 9
10 9 8 7 6 5 4 3 2 1

Editor: Elizabeth Brent
Design: Rocket Design (East Anglia) Ltd
Illustration: Alex Paterson. Illustration on 88–89 by Alan Irvine.

Wayland, an imprint of Hachette Children's Group
Part of Hodder & Stoughton
Carmelite House, 50 Victoria Embankment
London EC4Y 0DZ

Printed and bound by CPI Group (UK) Ltd, Coydon, CR0 4YY

Wayland is a division of Hachette Children's Books,
an Hachette UK company
www.hachette.co.uk

All illustrations by Shutterstock, except 4, 12, 14–15, 18, 23, 33, 41, 46–47, 52–53, 62–63, 68–69, 75, 76, 80, 88–89 and 92

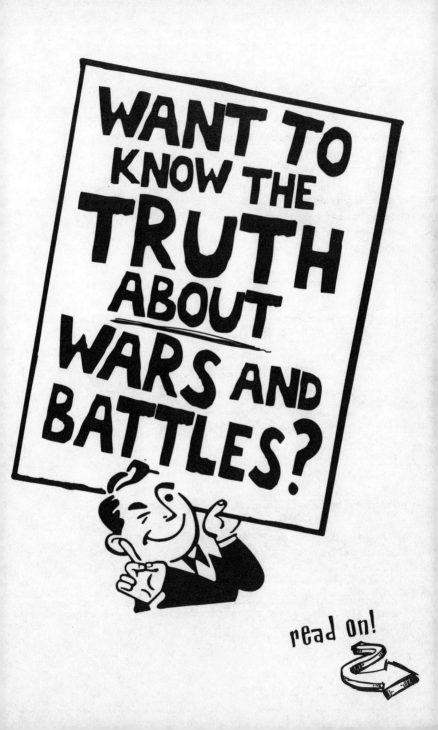

Read this bit first...!

Wars are GLORIOUS and FABULOUS events. They star brave, armour-clad knights, wielding swords and shields, who gallop into battle on horses with thundering hooves.

Right?

Er, wrong.

That's the romanticised version from long ago. In real life, wars and battles can be a lot dirtier and bloodier and deadlier. And unfortunately, because countries and kingdoms and people have always fallen out about who owns what bit of land and who should be wearing which crown and even who ate whose croissant — REALLY (see page 32) — there have been rather a lot of them. Remembrance Day reminds us of that.

So what are wars and battles really like? What about the brave souls who fight in them to defend their countries and their people? Why do wars kick off in the first place? What happens when things go horribly wrong...?

This book tells you what really happened in many of the most famous — and not-so-famous — wars and battles ever. But be prepared. Some of the things you may believe might not have happened exactly as you expected. Other gobsmacking facts about wars and battles might make you go...

Here's a quick quiz. Try to work out whether the following bizarre statements are true or false...

1. Soldiers rode into battle on 16-seater bicycles.

2. Lions once led donkeys into battle.

3. Roman gladiators fought with knives and forks.

Even though all this might sound bonkers, one of the above IS totally true. But guess what...? You're going to have to read the book to find out which one that is.

Murah ha ha

So prepare to be transported into the murk and mist of battlefields old and new, and be shocked and stunned by what did and didn't happen there. Things you always believed to be true might be blasted into infinity. Things that sound unbelievably silly might actually be true. Discover the daftest reasons to go to war and the oddest weapons ever invented. Bravest escapes? Check. Stupidest things ever said on a battlefield? That's here too. And much, much more...

read on!

So you might hear myths like...

> **Soldiers who survived the Crimean battlefield were safe and sound in Florence Nightingale's hospital**

When Russia invaded the Balkans, Britain, France and Turkey declared war on them and fighting erupted on the Crimean Peninsula (part of modern-day Ukraine). Those in charge thought that the Crimean War (1853–1856) would be a glorious war. The British Army was given a grand send-off and everyone thought that Russia would be beaten quickly and easily.

They couldn't have been more wrong.

> *Welcome to Scutari General. You're quite safe now, my dears*

Soldiers had to combat a terrible journey, lack of medical equipment, poor organisation and cholera. Oh, and the enemy. Any that were too ill to fight were shipped back to Scutari, to hospital.

Because hospitals are where people get better, right?

★ And the truth is...

The hospital in Scutari, where celebrity nurse Florence Nightingale worked, was the last place ANYONE should have been sent, and certainly not the sick and wounded.

It was a living hell. Thousands of patients were crowded into filthy, rat-infested corridors. Soldiers who survived injury on the battlefield then had to fight disease in the hospital. Many, many died.

Florence Nightingale tried her hardest to improve conditions at Scutari, but despite her best efforts, patients were STILL dying. During her first winter there, more than 4,000 soldiers died, and TEN TIMES more died from disease, rather than from battle wounds.

WHY?

The mystery was solved in 1855 when an investigation into the high death rate revealed that the hospital was built on top of old, rotting sewers. These were infecting both the water supply and the wards themselves. Once the sewers were cleared and the wards were properly ventilated, the death rate began to fall AT LAST.

Verdict: —— **BUSTED** ——

BATTLE BLUNDERS!

Lord Byron

This wasn't the Lord Byron who was the world-famous poet, of course. He was far too busy writing wonderful poetry to be bothered with the Battle of Marston Moor in 1644 (and he lived over a century later, which made it doubly impossible). No, although he was an ancestor of the poetic Byron, this was a different Lord completely.

So was he as brilliant in battle as his descendent was perfect at poetry?

Er, no.

During the Battle of Marston Moor, which was part of the First English

Civil War, Lord Byron was entrusted with guarding one flank of the Royalist army. Except, he got a bit bored of standing around and decided that it would be much more exciting to join in the battle.

So Lord Byron ordered his troops to get stuck in, leaving the part of the army they were supposed to be guarding UNGUARDED, which meant that Cromwell and his troops attacked.

And the Royalists lost.

So Lord Byron wasn't fabulous in battle at all. He was a bit of an idiot, actually.

Bombs don't bounce

Of course they don't bounce. Bombs have a heavy metal shell —
they're NOT made of rubber. Bombs are designed to explode on
impact, so that they destroy their target. So if you bounced
a bomb, you'd be history.

The very idea of a bouncing bomb is BONKERS...

★ And the truth is...

... unless your target is a dam during World War Two, of course.
Then, they're rather handy.

It's pretty difficult to destroy a dam with a traditional bomb.
And yet the Allies knew that if they blew up a series of dams
in Germany, they'd stand a better chance of winning the war.

So British aviation engineer Barnes Wallis set about designing
a drum-shaped, spinning bomb that could be dropped by an
aircraft flying towards the dam, and bounce on water until it
hit its target. It would sink to the bottom of the dam wall and
THEN explode, creating maximum damage.

It worked.

But Barnes Wallis felt forever guilty about the deaths his
invention caused.

Verdict: **BUSTED**

★ BONUS Bouncing-Bomb Fact

Barnes Wallis was NOT the first person to bounce bombs. That was Lord Horatio Nelson! He used to skim cannonballs across the waves – just like skimming stones – to hole enemy ships nearer the water line. This technique also gave the cannonballs greater OOMPH, making them even more deadly and dangerous.

Incoming!

Two countries once went to war over a golden stool

Get off!

★ And the truth is...

Actually, that's just what the Ashanti people of Africa's Gold Coast might have said when Sir Frederick Mitchell Hodgson, the British Governor, threatened to sit down on their hugely symbolic and very sacred golden stool.

As Hodgson was a foreigner, this was a very disrespectful thing to do and Yaa Asantewaa — queen mother of Ejisu in the Ashanti Empire — promptly led a rebellion against the British.

The British won. The Ashanti lost. But no one ever did sit on the golden stool.

Verdict:  TRUTH

The Light Brigade was a bunch of soldiers carrying torches

Well, that's what it sounds like, doesn't it?

⭐ **And the truth is...**

Sorry, no.

A brigade is a group of soldiers that forms part of a larger army. And a light brigade means that the soldiers aren't bristling with weaponry but are just lightly armed. They absolutely aren't illuminated.

Verdict: **BUSTED**

The term 'light brigade' became properly famous after Alfred Lord Tennyson wrote a poem called *The Charge of the Light Brigade*, which is about an ill-fated attack during the Crimean War (1853–1856). It starts like this...

> Half a league, half a league,
> Half a league onward,
> All in the valley of Death
> Rode the six hundred...

World War One tanks were named after water tanks

But that's ridiculous! Tanks look nothing like water tanks.

Water tanks are not metal fighting machines that thunder across battlefields on caterpillar tracks. They are not equipped with machine guns and a massive cannon. And they are definitely not armoured, to protect the soldiers inside from enemy gunfire. Water tanks just hold water. That's it.

GLUG

★ And the truth is...

Tanks really *were* named after water tanks. The British Army first used tanks on the battlefields of World War One. But no one wanted the enemy to guess what their brand new weapons were, so they pretended they were actually water tanks, supplying water to the troops.

The name stuck.

(Though the enemy probably figured out quite quickly that they weren't going to find water inside.)

SLOSH

DRINKING WATER

Verdict: ⎯⎯⎯ TRUTH ⎯⎯⎯

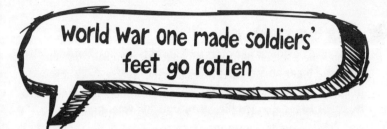

World War One made soldiers' feet go rotten

War is no laughing matter. Not only do soldiers battle each other, they also have to battle treacherous conditions too. But what sort of conditions could actually make a soldier's feet go rotten...?

⭐ And the truth is...

If you were a soldier fighting in the terrible, squelchy trenches of World War One, then there was a pretty good chance that you'd get trench foot. This was a condition where feet that had been standing in cold, wet, squishy, muddy conditions for long periods of time actually would start to go rotten. If treated properly, trench foot could be cured. If not, gangrene might set in and once that happened, the affected foot – or feet – could get the chop. Yikes.

Trench foot was first noticed in Napoleon's army in 1812, but it was also a problem in World Wars One and Two and in the Vietnam War.

⭐ BONUS FACT!

Believe it or not, festivalgoers from THIS century have also suffered from trench foot, when it rained heavily at music festivals, turning the ground into a quagmire. But as they were listening to music and not being shot at, it wasn't quite so much of a problem.

Verdict: ———— ————

19

> If you wanted to escape from Stalag Luft III, you needed a wooden horse

Stalag Luft III was a prisoner-of-war (POW) camp in Germany during World War Two, where a number of brave, fearless and very inventive Allied airmen took part in not one but TWO great escapes.

So did they use a wooden horse...?

★ And the truth is...

Yes. And no.

In 1943, the POWs hid the entrance to their escape tunnel under a wooden gymnastic vaulting horse. To disguise the sound of the airmen doing the digging, others vaulted over the horse.

Number of wooden horses: 1.

Number of escaped POWs: 3.

Number who succeeded: 3.

The same year, plans were hatched for an even more ambitious escape in which THREE tunnels — named Tom, Dick and Harry — were dug. Hundreds of POWs were involved in their construction. The Great Escape, as it became known, happened in March 1944, but ran into difficulties when the 77th escaped POW was spotted and the Gestapo gave chase.

Number of wooden horses: 0.

Number of escaped POWs: 77.

Number who succeeded: 3.

Verdict: _A little bit true but mostly_ **BUSTED**

> **Pssst!** If you want to find out more about either great escape, look out for these top, classic films: _The Wooden Horse_ (1950) and _The Great Escape_ (1963).

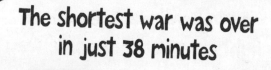

The shortest war was over in just 38 minutes

Pardon?

38 minutes?

It hardly seems long enough to fight a single battle, never mind to win or lose an entire war.

★ And the truth is...

It's absolutely true. That is exactly how long the Anglo-Zanzibar War lasted on 27 August 1896. (See? It was over so quickly that the war happened in a single day!)

The war occurred because the British weren't happy with the new sultan of Zanzibar. (They'd been best friends with the previous sultan and had already earmarked his successor.) So they asked Sultan Khalid bin Barghash to step down. Unsurprisingly, the sultan refused. Then he promptly called his troops to the palace and barricaded the doors.

When the British attacked, it took just 38 minutes for them to win.

It was officially the shortest war in history.

Verdict: —————— TRUTH ——————

During civil wars, everyone fights in a terribly polite way

That's what 'civil' means, doesn't it? If you're civil to someone, you're really well mannered.

★ And the truth is...

Well, yes. Except, if you're in a war situation, it actually means that the people doing the fighting all come from the same country.

Verdict: **BUSTED**

THEY INVENTED WHAT?

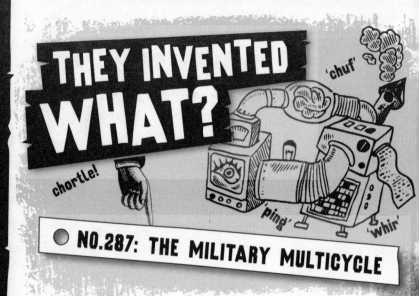

'chuf'

chortle!

'ping'

'whir'

○ NO.287: THE MILITARY MULTICYCLE

Do you need to transport eight, 12, 16 or more soldiers to a battlefield quickly and easily?

Is it 1887, the year before Karl Benz invented his motor car?

Are you potty about pedal power?

Then look no further — the military multicycle is the vehicle for you and your army. This vroomy velocipede is the very latest in pedal-powered transport. Link a collection of bicyles together, put two soldiers on each one, point them in the right direction and wish them luck as you wave them goodbye!

The Pros

 Environmentally friendly.

 Easy to steer — the cyclist on the front seat was in charge.

3 Suffered from less wind resistance than bicycles travelling one by one.

4 Top speed of 16 kilometres (or 10 miles) an hour.

Wow! Speedy!

The Cons

1 Everyone had to travel in the same direction.

2 It would have been a bone-shaking, bum-numbing ride...

3 ...and a good target for enemy fire too.

Did it catch on?

There were rumours that the multicycle would undergo rigorous testing ... and then no more was ever heard of it. So, no. It didn't catch on.

During World War One, lions were led into battle by donkeys

Pick those knees up! Left, right, left, right...

Huh?

Did animals REALLY take part in World War One?

⭐ And the truth is...

No, of course not.

Lions led by donkeys is a metaphor — a phrase that likens one thing to something else. It should not be taken literally. In this case, the **lions** (brave, strong, roaring creatures) are really the brave soldiers who fought in the war, while the **donkeys** (who have a terribly bad press as being silly beasts) are the idiot generals who kept sending soldiers over the top of the trenches to their deaths.

Verdict: The actual words are  but the meaning is TRUTH

In the Middle Ages, besieged castles were attacked with rotting animals

Erm, why? Wouldn't it be better to attack a super-sturdy castle with something a bit tougher, like a massive catapult or something? How totally BEASTLY.

★ And the truth is...

Besieged castles were pretty tricky to get into, and with good reason. They were designed that way. The whole point of a castle was to keep the people inside safe, and to keep the enemy outside.

As well as being impossibly sturdy, castles were built in hard-to-reach places too — on the top of hills or cliffs or surrounded by moats — making them particularly difficult to attack.

read on!

So how was the enemy supposed to get in?

Attackers had a few options...

They could push reeeeeeeally long ladders up against the outer walls. Then soldiers swarmed up the ladders, hoping to get inside the castle before they were pierced by arrows.

Going up!

They might smash a reeeeeeeeally big log — known as a battering ram — against the castle gate (or the walls), over and over again, until they bashed their way in.

Kerpow!

They could use catapults, crossbows and trebuchets (massive slings) to send rocks, arrows and other projectiles sailing over the walls to attack the people inside.

Peeeow!

Or they might lay siege to the castle, which meant cutting off all supplies and waiting until the castle occupants were so hungry that they surrendered.

Rumble Rumble

It's also totally true that the enemy DID try to speed things up a little by flinging rotten animals over the castle walls. This was a way of spreading infection and disease inside the castle, to force those under siege to give up. As well as disease-ridden — or just plain dead — animals, attackers catapulted actual human bodies over the walls too.

Ewwwwww.

Verdict: **TRUTH**

GERONIMO is just a word that army paratroopers shout to show they're not scared

Or parachutists.

Or bobsleighers.

Or bungee jumpers.

Or anyone who launches themselves into the unknown, really.

And the truth is...

'Geronimo' IS a word that parachutists are said to cry before launching themselves out of aircraft — both when they're jumping into battle and when they're skydiving for fun too.

> Geronimo!

But, it isn't *just* a word.

Geronimo was originally the nickname given to Native American war chief Mescalero-Chiricahua (1829–1909). He led battles against Mexico and the US during the Apache Wars, which happened because the two countries had taken land away from the Apache people. (It's not surprising Geronimo fought. His entire family was killed by enemy troops.) He surrendered to the US in 1886 and became a prisoner of war — and also a bit of a celebrity. Sadly, he was never allowed to return to his home.

'Geronimo' was first used as an exclamation in the 1940s when army troops had watched a film about the Apache chief's life and decided to shout it when they jumped, to show they weren't scared.

And it stuck.

Verdict: — **BUSTED** —

WEIRD WARS

THE PASTRY WAR

This bizarrely named war kicked off in 1838. French pastry chef Remontel claimed angrily that his shop in Mexico City had been attacked and looted by Mexican officers. (Presumably they then ate all the pies and the croissants and the rest of the pastry products that Remontel was selling.)

When the Mexican government ignored the outraged Remontel, the pastry chef appealed to his own country to sort things out. The French had already loaned Mexico A LOT of money, which they hadn't paid back, so this made them even more cross and they demanded EVEN MORE money from Mexico.

The Mexicans didn't pay up.

So, the French sent a fleet of ships to blockade all Mexican ports. They bombarded the fortress of San Juan de Ulúa. They also seized the port of Veracruz. Oh, and they nabbed the Mexican Navy too.

Unsurprisingly, Mexico declared war on France.

Then the old Mexican president — Santa Anna — decided to join in the bun fight. (Though everyone seemed to have forgotten all about the pastry by now.) He led the Mexicans against the French. He lost his leg, but gained huge amounts of publicity because of his injury and was made president once more.

It was at this point that the British decided it was time everyone made friends again. They persuaded the Mexicans to pay damages to the pastry chef and the French forces to go home.

The Pastry War was over.

Elephants are excellent warriors

Tamerlane was a Turkic ruler — also known as Timur the Lame — who conquered much of Asia in the fourteenth century. But he knew quite a bit about elephants too.

So he must have known that elephants would be great in a war situation, right?

Charge!

I want my mummy!

⭐ And the truth is...

Wrong.

Tamerlane knew that the Indian war elephants his armies faced were SCARY, but he also knew that they panicked easily, so he loaded his camels with wood and hay, and set this alight. Then he sent the frantic, fiery and VERY LOUD (well, they were on fire — no wonder they were loud) creatures charging towards the elephants. It worked. The elephants panicked and ran. (But what a nasty thing to do to elephants AND camels...)

Verdict: — **BUSTED** — They so aren't. NEVER take an elephant to war.

WEIRD WARS

THE FOOTBALL WAR

In 1969, El Salvador and Honduras went to war after a football match. It wasn't totally because of the football match. Things were already very tense between the two countries. But it all kicked off (GEDDIT?) before a vital qualifying round for the 1970 World Cup, when El Salvador severed diplomatic relations with Honduras. The football match was still played, but afterwards fans rioted. Then, a few days later on 14 July, El Salvador attacked Honduras and fierce fighting went on until 18 July, when the ceasefire was sorted.

It was also known as the 100 Hour War, for obvious reasons.

The Greeks used magic spells to set boats on fire

Wow. Actual magic? That's some secret weapon.

★ And the truth is...

No, of course not. But Greek Fire was just as mysterious as magic. It was an explosive mixture that was launched at enemy ships and, on impact, set them on fire.

Greek Fire MAY have included some or all or none of the following ingredients:

PINE RESIN (sticky stuff that comes from pine trees)

NAPHTHA (flammable oil that comes from coal, shale or petroleum)

QUICKLIME (white substance made by heating limestone)

SULPHUR (a yellow crystal-like chemical that catches fire easily)

POTASSIUM NITRATE (a silvery chemical)

HUMMUS*

But we'll never know what Greek Fire was made of, because the secret recipe was lost...

Verdict: —— **BUSTED** ——

* Ha ha ha ha ha! No. This is, of course, a trick Greek ingredient to see if you're paying attention. You are. Well done.

A war was once lost because of a missing horseshoe nail

Or so says the famous poem, anyway...

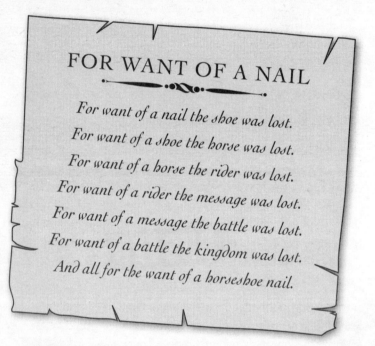

FOR WANT OF A NAIL

For want of a nail the shoe was lost.
For want of a shoe the horse was lost.
For want of a horse the rider was lost.
For want of a rider the message was lost.
For want of a message the battle was lost.
For want of a battle the kingdom was lost.
And all for the want of a horseshoe nail.

So there you go. A nail once fell out of a horseshoe and — because it wasn't banged back in again — a kingdom was lost.

And the truth is...

There probably never was a war where events happened exactly as they do in the rhyme. It's a proverb, which is a wise saying that warns people in all sorts of situations – not just war – that tiny mistakes can have huge consequences. (Scientists also call this the butterfly effect, which describes the way that the tiniest random flutter of a butterfly's wings has an effect on something else, which has an effect on something else, which eventually results in something HUGE happening on the other side of the world. Like a hurricane or something. Wow.)

Anyway, the lesson that this particular proverb is teaching is that if your horse has a nail missing from his shoe, you'd better pop another one in there pretty quickly, or else...

Verdict:

THEY INVENTED WHAT?

'chuf'

chortle!

'ping'

'whir'

○ NO.2067: THE HELMET GUN

Just imagine. You're in the middle of the battlefield and you want to protect your head from enemy fire, but you want to fire a gun at the same time. What do you DO?

Er... how about wearing a helmet on your head and holding a gun in your hands? Too obvious?

Don't worry! Albert Bacon Pratt of Vermont in the USA solved this problem way back in 1916, when he invented — and patented — his fabulous helmet gun!

Featuring a gun barrel at the front of the helmet, the wearer aimed by turning their head until they were facing the target. Then all they had to do was blow down a tube, connected to a bulb that, when inflated, pressed the trigger to fire the helmet gun.

BOOM!

The Pros

1 Fire a gun AND protect your head.

2 Keep your hands free to hold other weaponry.

3 No messing about with gunsights — just look at the target to aim!

The Cons

1 Although Pratt claimed to have solved the problem of recoil, science suggests that if you fire a gun with your head, the force is probably going to mean that your actual head is pushed in the opposite direction. (Just ask Isaac Newton. This is pretty much what his third law of motion says.) Ow.

Did it catch on?

No.

> # World War One ended on the 11th day of the 11th month, at 11am PRECISELY

11 November

What a HUGE coincidence that everyone stopped fighting at such a precise time. Did it *really* happen like that?

⭐ And the truth is...

Yes, it did.

It wasn't a coincidence, of course. The exact time that war between the Allies and Germany would cease was decided beforehand, so why not pick a memorable time? But the important thing was that after four long years of war and millions of deaths, fighting stopped at last.

Verdict: **TRUTH**

More true facts about the Armistice

1. The agreement that ended World War One was called the Armistice.

2. It was signed in a railway carriage, in a forest.

3. Armistice means 'stoppage'.

4. King George V decided that 11 November should be called Armistice Day, when everyone would remember those who died in the war.

5. After the end of World War Two in 1945, Armistice Day became known as Remembrance Day, to remember those who died in both world wars.

OK gentlemen, it's time.

Ancient Greek armies were square

Oh dear.

square *(adj.)* old-fashioned and boring

How disappointing! Ancient Greek soldiers seemed the very opposite of square. Weren't they terribly dashing in their metal breastplates and shiny shin pads and plumed helmets?

And the truth is...

Ancient Greek foot soldiers — known as hoplites — did look fabulous. But it's true that the armies in which they fought *were* square. Or rather, the individual groups of soldiers who made up an army went into battle in a square formation. A phalanx had 16 rows, each with 16 hoplites in them. So, there were 16 x 16 soldiers, which makes 256 in total, which you will have worked out WAY before now, using your 16 times table.

It was all VERY organised.

The first five rows of hoplites approached the enemy with their 6.5-metre-long spears pointing forward. This meant that the hoplites could poke the enemy before they even got there.

The hoplites in the rear rows held their spears upright, so as not to get in the way. (You wouldn't want to poke your fellow foot soldiers accidentally. They might get a bit cross.) But as soldiers fell in front of them, the hoplites at the back lowered their own spears to make sure that there was always a prickly reception for the enemy.

Hoplites were citizen-soldiers, and were primarily free citizens, such as farmers and craftsmen, rather than slaves. This was because they had to buy their own armour which, made of solid bronze as it was, did not come cheap.

Verdict:

The Battle of Marathon inspired the modern-day race

Way back in 490BCE, it wasn't looking good for the Greeks at the Battle of Marathon. Hugely outnumbered by Persian soldiers, they needed help, FAST. So it's said that Greek messenger Pheidippides ran first to Sparta to ask for help — a round trip of about 240 km, or 150 miles — and then, when the Greeks had triumphed over the Persians, ran all the way to Athens to announce the victory. That journey was 26 miles and 385 yards long, which is just over 42 km.

And then it's said that poor Pheidippides dropped dead from exhaustion.

So the marathon was invented to commemorate his superhuman effort.

★ And the truth is...

Except, although a lot of people have written about this story since — including Robert Browning in the nineteenth century, who penned a poem about Pheidippides — every version can be traced back to just the one source. And historians aren't *totally* sure that it's true.

All the same, marathons are now run all over the world to remember the Ancient Greek's jaw-dropping deed, whether he did it or not. And the official length of each marathon is 26 miles and 385 yards, the same distance run by Pheidippides (probably).

Nice shorts!

So whether Pheidippides's marathon was a story or a true fact doesn't really matter. The modern marathon is run because of the Battle of Marathon.

Verdict: TRUTH

47

BATTLE BLUNDERS!

John Sedgwick

Major General John Sedgwick was a Union Army general in the American Civil War who spoke too soon.

At the Battle of Spotsylvania Court House, he inspected his troops, who were just under a kilometre away from enemy snipers, safely out of sight of the whizzing bullets.

Sedgwick was HORRIFIED at their cowardliness. He gave his troops a huge, shouty ticking off and told them to stand up and fight.

They didn't move. (They weren't daft.)

So Sedgwick told them he was ASHAMED of them.

They still didn't move.
(They still weren't daft.)

'They couldn't hit an elephant at this distance!' cried Sedgwick.

He was promptly shot dead by a sniper.

Psst!

The bullet hit Sedgwick just below his left eye. So the enemy snipers – or sharpshooters, as they were then known – were a pretty good shot after all. And the chances are, they could have hit an elephant.

Ouch!

Welsh women beat Napoleon's troops

Women now fight on the front line of battles, but it wasn't always like this. The USA, for example, only lifted the ban on women serving in combat positions in 2013.

So how can Welsh women possibly have beaten Napoleon's troops two hundred years earlier...?

★ And the truth is...

Napoleon's troops were usually quite good at fighting (they had a lot of practice) but the last time they invaded the British Isles in 1797, they didn't make a brilliant job of it.

First, local woman Jemima Nicholas captured a dozen French troops *on her own*.

Then, a group of Welsh women marched towards the troops, who mistook them for soldiers (to be fair, they were wearing red coats and black hats, so from a distance they may have looked SLIGHTLY as though they were in uniform) and surrendered.

Game over.

Verdict:  TRUTH

> ## Sea commanders are never seasick

Of course they're never seasick. They are too busy commanding their crews and winning famous sea battles to have time to be sick.

★ And the truth is...

Actually, Rear-Admiral Lord Horatio Nelson, who had a starring role in the Napoleonic Wars, was probably the greenest sailor of them all. He secretly confessed his terrible seasickness in a letter to a friend: 'I am ill every time it blows hard and nothing but my enthusiastic love for the profession keeps me one hour at sea.'

Which makes his victory at the Battle of Trafalgar — on board the HMS *Victory* — even more heroic, really.

Verdict: **BUSTED**

In the movie version of Shakespeare's *Henry V* (1944), legendary actor Sir Laurence Olivier, wearing a full suit of armour, is hoisted into his saddle by a crane.

So it must be true, because film makers are hardly going to get such a huge historical detail wrong, are they?

★ And the truth is...

If armour were so heavy that a knight couldn't climb onto a horse, then it would be too heavy to fight in too.

Back in Henry V's day, armour-clad knights simply popped a foot in the horse's stirrup and hoisted their other leg over the saddle, exactly how people usually get onto a horse. They didn't need a crane to help them.

The crane confusion seems to have begun during the late-nineteenth century, possibly as a joke. And even though a top historian objected to the use of the crane in *Henry V*, he was ignored.

Verdict: ___ BUSTED ___

Heave!

WEIRD WARS

THE PIG AND POTATO WAR

This peculiar war took place in 1859 on the San Juan Islands, which are situated between Vancouver Island and the North American mainland.

Here's what happened...

An American farmer called Lyman Cutlar, who'd claimed land on the San Juan Islands, found a pig eating his potatoes.

Cutlar shot the pig.

The unfortunate pig was owned by an Irishman called Charles Griffin. Cutlar offered him $10 compensation for the loss of his pig, but Griffin wanted $100.

Then Cutlar decided that the pig was trespassing, which meant that he shouldn't have to pay any compensation at all.

The British threatened to arrest Cutlar, so he in turn asked the US to help.

The US sent 66 soldiers to lend a hand.

The British sent three battleships.

So the US sent another 395 soldiers.

And the British sent another two battleships and boosted their total number of soldiers to a whopping 2,140.

Meanwhile, those in charge decided that really, this was a very silly way to behave over a pig and both sides were told that they must NOT fire the first shot.

So no one did.

And no one was hurt.

Except for the pig, of course. No one saved his bacon.

Mmmm, nice spuds!

Vikings wore horns on their helmets to scare the enemy

Think about it. Have you EVER seen a Viking without horns?

⭐ And the truth is...

Wow! You've seen a real, true-life Viking? Or... have you seen a million fancy-dress Vikings? Because they're a TINY bit different. (And lived about a thousand years later than the original Vikings.)

Real-life Viking warriors actually wore plain conical helmets made of leather and stiffened with wood and metal, while the chieftains wore more protective metal helmets. Apart from some historical references to Vikings wearing helmets with horns — or antlers or wings — during religious ceremonies, there's no evidence that other Vikings wore them.

It was during Victorian times that the idea of horned helmets became popular. The myth is still believed today, which is why you'll usually see a fancy-dress Viking wearing horns.

Verdict: **BUSTED**

Blood grooves in swords are there to make a victim bleed faster

A blood groove — or a 'fuller', as it is more properly called — is a groove that runs the length of a sword, knife or bayonet blade. Many believe that when the blade was plunged into the enemy's body (OUCH), the groove helped blood to flow more quickly and easily from the victim.

★ And the truth is...

A blood groove is simply there to make the blade lighter. A bevelled or rounded groove does not make a sword or other weapon weaker, but it does make it a lot easier to wave around. And it uses less metal, too, so it's cheaper.

It has absolutely nothing to do with blood.

Verdict: **BUSTED**

Lawrence of Arabia was from Arabia

T. E. Lawrence's top war skills made him a Very Important Person during the Arab Revolt* of 1916. He advised the son of the revolt's leader, Sherif Hussein of Mecca, on tactics. But he wasn't just involved behind the scenes. He was on the front line, too, attacking Turkish communications and supplies. His war efforts made Lawrence quite the celebrity. He was so famous that he earned the nickname Lawrence of Arabia.

So he *came* from Arabia, right?

* This happened when Arabs fought back against the Turkish rulers who'd been in charge for centuries.

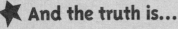

⭐ And the truth is...

Er, no.

Lawrence of Arabia was actually from North Wales.

Thomas Edward Lawrence was born in the Welsh village of Tremadog in 1888. He studied history at Oxford University and went on to become an archaeologist in the Middle East. He trained as a soldier, too, and when World War One broke out, he was recruited by the British Army as a spy. (Shhhhh.)

His exploits in World War One made Lawrence of Arabia famous — he was even given a job by Winston Churchill — but he wasn't keen on being a celeb. He hated it, in fact. So Lawrence spent the rest of his life trying to hide from the world, working in the RAF and Tank Corps under fake names. He died in 1935 after a motorbike accident, but became famous all over again in 1962 when the film *Lawrence of Arabia* was released, starring Peter O'Toole. To find out more, watch the film!

Verdict: — **BUSTED** —

THEY INVENTED WHAT?

'chuf'

chortle!

'ping'

'whir'

○ NO.899: THE CIRCULAR BATTLESHIP

Bored of regular-shaped battleships?

Would you rather sail to war in something just a little bit different?

Then check out the *Novgorod*, for all your barmy battleship needs!

This Russian warship was designed by Andrei Alexandrovich Popov — and was nicknamed a popovka after him. Launched in 1873, it was 30.8 metres long... and 30.8 metres wide. That's not a typo. The hull was CIRCULAR, when viewed from above.

The Pros

1. It was, um, really inventive and different!

2. Er, that's it, actually.

The Cons

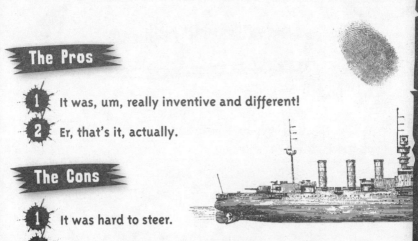

1. It was hard to steer.

2. It was said to be 'the ugliest warship ever built'.

3. It pitched (the bow moved up and down) and rolled (swayed from side to side) A LOT, even when the sea wasn't very rough.

Bleurgh!

Did it catch on?

No. Both the Novgorod and its sister ship, the Rear Admiral Popov, were scrapped in 1912. Meanwhile, battleships continue to be built in the traditional pointy style.

Soldiers wear make-up

Pah. As if soldiers have got time to be putting on make-up in a war situation.

Great outfit... I saw you, um, miles away!

★ And the truth is...

Actually, make-up can help save a soldier's life. It's not normal make-up, of course. It's face paint that acts as camouflage, helping soldiers to blend in with their surroundings and hide from enemies. They wear camouflaged clothes, too, to match.

Soldiers daub themselves with different colours depending on their habitat. For example, it wouldn't make much sense to wear a leafy green if you were fighting in the Arctic.

Verdict: TRUTH

Camouflage paint now contains insect repellent, to help soldiers hide from pesky mosquitoes too.

Pssst! Modern camouflage can even protect the wearer from the really high temperatures given off by explosions and fire, giving them vital extra seconds to escape before they suffer burns.

Māori warriors danced on the battlefield

Really? This is hardly a time to be waltzing.

★ And the truth is...

The Māori warriors of New Zealand didn't waltz, of course, but they *did* perform the haka on the battlefield. This is an ancient dance, designed to show the enemy how strong and powerful the warriors are. A haka might include: chanting, shouting, grunting, hand slapping, feet stamping and tongue poking.

But did you know that a haka isn't just a war dance? It could also be used when the two sides made friends, making it a peace dance too. (And a welcoming dance and a special-occasion dance and a funeral dance.)

Verdict: ___ TRUTH ___

PSSST!
You can often see the haka being performed by the New Zealand national rugby team — the All Blacks. It's VERY scary.

WEIRD WARS

THE DOG TAX WAR

This took place in New Zealand during the nineteenth century. The county council (run by the British) had the brilliant idea of levying a dog tax on each dog. The local Māoris refused to pay. They said that if dogs were taxed, people would be next. And as it was their country in the first place, they really didn't want that to happen.

So there was a brief war. (Yikes.)

And then there was a truce. (Phew.)

But the good news was that no one was hurt. (Hurray!)

Even though the dog tax remains, no one really pays any attention to it. Although people ARE taxed, just as the Māoris warned.

Hmmph

Napoleon planned to invade the UK via a channel tunnel

I've got loads of GREAT ideas!

How forward-thinking of the French emperor! Fancy Napoleon Bonaparte deciding to build a tunnel beneath the English Channel nearly two hundred years before it actually opened.

And the truth is...

Yes. Yes, he did. Except Napoleon's tunnel was never built because it was too difficult a task for the nineteenth century. (They hadn't invented tunnel-boring machines, for a start.)

But that didn't put Napoleon off. He came up with another plan to invade Britain by sea and, in preparation for an attack, improved port facilities at Boulogne massively. But a trial run ended VERY badly and lots of soldiers were lost. So he gave up on that idea too.

And then there was his totally wacky plan of using hot-air balloons to float his troops across the English Channel. But that idea never took off. (Geddit? Never took off?! Oh, never mind.)

It was also rumoured that he was going to send a huge raft of soldiers to invade Britain.

Dang, the wind's changed direction again!

He didn't.

On the British side of the English Channel, however, Napoleon's threats did inspire improvements to fortifications along the south coast. So if Napoleon had reached The Other Side, there's no guarantee he would have won there anyway.

Verdict: ⎯⎯⎯ ★TRUTH★ ⎯⎯⎯

Trench warfare is one of the muddiest and bloodiest types of fighting ever. In World War One, an army's front line was a muddy trench in which soldiers sheltered from enemy gunfire. The enemy's front line was on the far side of an area called No Man's Land. This was because it belonged to no one. And this was where the actual fighting took place.

read on!

An army advanced by sending soldiers over the top of their trench into No Man's Land and straight into the line of fire. They also had to avoid barbed wire, mortars, flamethrowers, the newly invented machine gun and the TRULY DESPICABLE mustard gas, which caused terrible burns. Any soldiers lucky enough to survive would try to break through the enemy's front line. Then it all started all over again, the two front lines moving back and forth, depending on who was winning.

So what about the football match? If No Man's Land was such a dangerous, frightening, muddy place to be, HOW could soldiers play football there together?

★ And the truth is...

On Christmas Eve 1914, something amazing happened in the battlefields of Ypres. First, Allied and German soldiers sang carols in their own trenches. Then a German soldier walked across the battlefield to suggest a ceasefire. The Allies agreed and soldiers from the two armies met in No Man's Land and shook hands. The two sides recovered their fallen comrades from the battlefield. And THEN a ball appeared and the two sides played a peaceful game of football together.

The truce lasted only a few days and was never repeated.

But Christmas 1914 was one to remember.

Verdict: ———— TRUTH ————

70

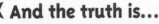

In the Crimean war, soldiers had two left feet

Wow. They must have been TERRIBLE dancers.

★ And the truth is...

Of course not. But it would have been more useful if they HAD had two left feet because it's rumoured that a boatload of boots which arrived in the Crimea were ALL made for left feet.

The right-footed boots were supposedly on a different ship.

They must have been kicking themselves.

HOWEVER, there is a chance that the left-boot incident was made up by inventive Victorians, who were responsible for the claim that Vikings wore horns* on their helmets too. So maybe the story isn't true after all.

Although we can be reasonably certain that soldiers in the Crimea didn't have two left feet either. Just in case you weren't sure.

Verdict:  * See page 56.

71

THEY INVENTED WHAT?

'chuf'

chortle!

'ping'

'whir'

○ NO.273: THE BAT BOMB

Q. What do you get if you cross a bomb with a bat?

A. A bomb bat!

Erm, no... That would be ridiculous. Try again?

A. A bat bomb!

CORRECT.

The bat bomb was an actual invention that involved strapping small bombs to poor, unsuspecting bats and then sending them on a deadly mission.

Developed in the US, a canister containing about ONE THOUSAND hibernating bats would be flown to a great height over the target area ... and then dropped. But don't worry. The bats didn't fall to their deaths. The plummeting canister's descent was slowed by a parachute and the theory was that as the outside temperature warmed up, the bats would awaken. When the canister had dropped to a height of about 300 metres, it would open, releasing the bats. Their job was to fly to the nearest building and find a nice cosy spot under the eaves. Then, at exactly the same time, the mini bombs would EXPLODE, taking the poor, poor bats with them.

The Pros

 1 No one would suspect an innocent-looking bat of carrying a bomb.

2 One thousand bats could scatter over quite a wide area, destroying many buildings at the same time.

The Cons

 1 It was hardly very fair on the bats.

 2 It was very, very expensive, costing a total of $2 million.

Did it catch on?

No. When bomb-laden bats were released by accident in 1943, they decided to camp out UNDER A FUEL TANK at an army air base in New Mexico, USA. BOOM. The project never really got going after this, and it was cancelled when those in charge heard that it would not be ready until 1945 – the year that World War Two ended.

Joan of Arc was executed because she dressed as a man

SAINT Joan of Arc is a French heroine. When she was 12, she said that God had told her to go and fight. He'd also told her to cut her hair short and wear men's clothing. So she did. And during the Hundred Years War (see page 88), she became a captain in the French army, leading them to victory at many important battles. Unfortunately, Joan was captured and burned at the stake by the English when she was just 19 years old.

⭐ And the truth is...

Women's clothing in the fifteenth century would've really got in the way when Joan was fighting, so it's not surprising she wore men's clothes, even if she hadn't heard God telling her to do so. They were MUCH more practical.

But at her trial, Joan of Arc was charged with heresy (beliefs that are the total opposite of what most people think), sorcery (magic) and wearing men's clothes. Yes, really. That was a crime. And because they couldn't make any of the other charges stick, Joan of Arc WAS sentenced to death because of her clothes. How BONKERS is that?

Verdict:

74

Grenadiers wore bearskin hats to pretend they were taller

Ha ha!

As if a tall hat would fool ANYONE.

★ And the truth is...

Absolutely. The high fur hats worn by the British, Spanish and French in the eighteenth century were hardly practical for the battlefield. But what they were good for was making the wearer look Very Grand and also Very Tall. (And Very Silly.)

These hats are still worn by troops in Belgium, Canada, Denmark, Italy, the Netherlands, Sweden and the UK — but not on the battlefield. They are strictly for ceremonial occasions only.

Verdict:  TRUTH

The Cold War was fought in the Arctic Circle

And where else would you fight a cold war, if not somewhere COLD?

★ And the truth is...

No, it wasn't. There wasn't even any actual fighting. The Cold War referred more to the cold atmosphere that existed between the US and the Soviet Union — or USSR — after World War Two. Frosty relations continued until 1991, when the Soviet Union officially broke up into separate countries and Mikhail Gorbachev — the last Soviet leader, who did much to reform the country and bring about peace — resigned.

Verdict:

King Harold died when an arrow hit him in the eye

The Battle of Hastings in 1066 is where Anglo-Saxon king Harold II was struck in the eye by an arrow. He lost his life, his throne and his country, all in one go. William II of Normandy was the victor and became William the Conqueror. (Not that he wanted to rub anyone's nose in it or anything.) Or at least, that's how the story goes.

★ And the truth is...

No one is actually sure how Harold died. It MIGHT have been because of an arrow in the eye, but this was not an eye-witness story. (Geddit? Eye witness?!) In fact, this story was first recorded 14 years after the battle by an Italian monk. It's unlikely that he was at the Battle of Hastings. The Bayeux Tapestry — a very famous and very looooooong tapestry that records the entire battle — is confusing. Underneath the caption saying that Harold has been killed, there are two soldiers: one with an arrow in his eye and the other being pierced by a sword. We don't know which one is Harold.

Verdict: Possibly TRUTH but most likely BUSTED

77

Hitler wanted to blow up the Eiffel Tower

Really? Hitler wanted to send the most famous landmark in Paris sky high?

Quel horreur!

⭐ And the truth is...

Oui.

Adolf Hitler *did* want to demolish the Eiffel Tower during World War Two, while the Nazis were occupying the French capital. (Just think of all that handy iron he could use to make weapons and other war paraphernalia.) Luckily, his orders were never carried out.

The Parisians had the last laugh when the French Resistance — a secret army of French citizens — cut the cables to the Eiffel Tower's lifts, just before the Nazi leader was due to visit. This meant that if he'd wanted to admire the view, Hitler would've had to climb 1,710 steps.

Hitler had a choice: climb 1,710 steps or not.

He gave it a miss ... and the Eiffel Tower is still standing.

Verdict: _____ TRUTH _____

79

To lose one horse would be unlucky.

To lose two horses would be unfortunate.

To lose THREE horses would be downright CARELESS. Was the Earl really that hopeless at looking after his horses?

★ **And the truth is...**

Yes.

But sadly, it wasn't just three of the Earl of Uxbridge's horses that fell on the battlefield. It was more... After his first horse was shot, the Earl went back into battle on another poor animal. Again and again and again. It was while he was sitting on the eighth or ninth horse — unsurprisingly, they lost count — that the Earl's luck ran out and he and his steed were on the receiving end of a cannonball. The Earl lost his leg. It is not known what happened to the horse, but it probably wasn't a happy ending.

Neigh!

Verdict: **BUSTED**

Turn over to find out what happened to the Earl's leg!

...and then the Earl's leg became a tourist attraction

Eh?

Since when did sawn-off limbs compete with Buckingham Palace and the Statue of Liberty as a fun thing to go and see on holiday? What's next? A sausage museum? A parasite museum? A museum of famous dog collars?!*

RIP the Earl of Uxbridge's Leg

And the truth is...

In 1815, that's when.

After the Earl's right leg was blasted away, surgeons sawed off his leg above the knee. (They didn't use antiseptic or anaesthetic. Ouch.) The operation was carried out in the village of Waterloo, at the home of a certain Monsieur Paris. Afterwards, Paris had a rather strange request...

Could he please bury the leg in his garden and then turn the leg grave into a sort of shrine, with its own tombstone?

The Earl said YES. (Or maybe OUI.)

Everyone who was anyone came to gawp. Even the King of Prussia visited. And they all paid Monsieur Paris an entrance fee, so he was very happy.

As for the Earl — who was now a Marquess — someone made him a fabulous hinged artificial leg. His actual leg was buried with Uxbridge after he died and they were reunited, at last.

Verdict:

* Actually, these are all real-life museums too. The Currywurst (a type of German sausage) Museum is in Berlin, Germany. You can learn all about gruesome parasites in Tokyo. And if dog collars are your thing, take a trip to Leeds Castle in Kent, England.

Archimedes
HEY INVENTED WHAT?

'chuf'

chortle!

'ping'

'whir'

Archimedes

That's him!

Archimedes of Syracuse (c287 BCE – c212 BCE) wasn't just a Greek mathematical genius. (And a physicist and an engineer and an inventor and an astronomer.) He came in handy in a war situation too.

Here are just three of the fabulous weapons that he might (or might not) have invented.

PSSST! Because Archimedes lived such a long time ago, records of his battle inventions are a little sketchy. Historians are not 100% sure if he did invent them or not. But wouldn't it be fabulous if he had...?

The Death Ray

Devilishly simple in its design, the death ray was a bunch of mirrors that reflected the sun's light, focusing the beams onto a single point on the enemy ship, which became hotter and hotter until it BURST INTO FLAMES ... and then sank.

PSSSt! Instead of actual mirrors, experts think that the Death Ray would have used VERY shiny shields made of bronze or copper. Because they were curved, the rays of sunlight would have been even hotter.

ZAP!

FIZZZZZZZ......

The Death Ray!

Arghh, what's that?

read on!

The Iron Claw

Just imagine if your Greek city were being attacked by enemy ships... Wouldn't you just love to get your hands on a crane that could pluck Roman ships out of the sea?

Archimedes had the very same idea. He is said to have invented an ingenious device that was a cross between a crane and a many-pointed hook. When lowered into the sea, it was designed to bite into the enemy ship, capturing it. The crane would then be used to hoist the ship out of the water and drop back into the sea, to sink. Or simply to tip the vessel over. Just like that.

The Catapult

Actually, Archimedes didn't invent the catapult, which is a device that flings projectiles a long way, but he's said to have used it to great effect in a war situation.

Perhaps you've made your own catapult using a forked stick and an elastic band to twang small objects short distances? (Well done. Hopefully you didn't hit any priceless Ming vases or siblings.) Archimedes' catapult system was similar, but it could hurl rocks, lumps of wood and other random objects (all of them heavy and designed to inflict maximum damage) huuuuuuuuuge distances. This meant that soldiers could attack enemy ships in the harbour from the safety of their walled city.

An 'old-school' catapult

The Hundred Years War lasted for one hundred years

Well, it's hardly going to be called the Hundred Years War if it lasted for, say, 116 years, is it?

★ And the truth is...

The Hundred Years War lasted for 116 years.

The English king Edward III started it all in 1337. When his uncle, Charles IV of France, died, he thought that he should become king of France too. But the French wanted Charles' cousin Philip to be king. So they fought. And fought. Again and again and again. When the kings died, it didn't even signal an end to the fighting. Their successors simply carried on the war.

The Battle of Agincourt, starring Henry V, was one of the most famous battles of the Hundred Years War.

Watch it!

But there were many more. And by the time it was over and the French had won, Edward III had been dead for 76 years.

Verdict: BUSTED

Spartacus and his fellow slaves fought with cutlery

Eh? So what did they do? EAT their enemies?

I NEVER go into battle without an egg whisk

⭐ And the truth is...

No, not really. They were rebel slaves, not cannibals.

Spartacus had once been a Roman soldier, but was sold into slavery and sent to gladiator school near Mount Vesuvius. This was so he could learn how to fight (sometimes to the death) to entertain crowds of Romans. Unsurprisingly, Spartacus didn't fancy this, so he decided to make a run for it, along with two hundred other slaves. They DID use kitchen tools to escape, but history doesn't reveal whether this was knives, forks, spoons, cheese graters or something a bit more useful in a battle situation.

Verdict: **BUSTED**

WEIRD WARS

THE EMU WAR

The Emu War took place in 1932, when emus were running riot in the Australian Desert, gobbling crops and upsetting farmers. There were so many emus — about 20,000 — that the authorities decided something major was needed to sort them out.

So they sent in soldiers.

It was WAR.

Except, the emus turned out to be much better at avoiding machine-gun fire than anyone expected. Faced with soldiers who were laden down with equipment, the emus simply ran away. After a week, just 2,500 emus had been killed.

Take cover guys, it's the army!

The ceasefire came when the soldiers realised they would never win.

Boudicca — or Boadicea as she is also known — was the Celtic queen of the Iceni tribe, who lived in East Anglia in England. She lived in the first century AD and famously led a successful uprising against the Romans, who were then occupying Britain. After victories in Colchester, London and St Albans, Boudicca was defeated, but had the last laugh — sort of — when she swallowed poison rather than be captured. But this is not how people remember her. Boudicca appears in paintings — and in a statue in Westminster, London — riding into battle on a horse-drawn chariot with REALLY POINTY scythes attached to the wheels, clutching an EQUALLY POINTY spear.

Scary, huh?

 ## And the truth is...

This is how the Victorians — who discovered ancient writings that told of Boudicca's victories — imagined that the Celtic queen looked. They didn't actually know. And it's likely that they might have romanticised her image just a little bit. For all we know, she might have fought on foot. This isn't the only myth put forward about the warrior queen, either. In the 1930s, despite there being absolutely NO historical evidence whatsoever, the rumour circulated that Boudicca was buried between platforms 9 and 10 of Kings Cross station, in London!

Verdict: Probably

but who can say? Wouldn't it be great if it were the truth...?

Where can I find myths about...

100%
SUCKER-PROOF

GUARANTEED!

Take a look at our other marvellously mythbusting titles...

Tip: Turn over!